Getting To Know...

Nature's Children

COYOTE

Caroline Greenland

SCHOLASTIC INC.

New York Toronto London Auckland Sydney
Mexico City New Delhi Hong Kong Buenos Aires

Facts in Brief

Classification of the Coyote

Class: *Mammalia* (mammals)
Order: *Carnivora* (meat-eaters)
Family: *Canidae* (dog family)
Genus: *Canis*
Species: *Canis latrans*

World distribution. Exclusive to North and Central America. Found from Panama through western North America, up into Alaska.

Habitat. Plains and lightly wooded areas; have also adapted to forests, bushlands, and tundra.

Distinctive physical characteristics. Bushy tail; large pointed ears; slender muzzle; yellowish-gray fur.

Habits. Mates for life; active mainly at night; sometimes hunts in packs; noted for eerie howl that usually is heard at dusk and dawn, but also at night.

Diet. Mainly small animals; sometimes birds, deer, pronghorns, insects, and vegetation.

Revised edition copyright © 2001 by Scholastic Inc.
Original material © 1985 Grolier Limited.
All rights reserved.

Published by Scholastic Inc.
90 Old Sherman Turnpike, Danbury, Connecticut 06816.

SCHOLASTIC and associated logos are trademarks of Scholastic Inc.

ISBN 0-7172-6706-7

Printed in the U.S.A.

Edited by: Elizabeth Grace Zuraw
Photo Rights: Ivy Images

Photo Editor: Nancy Norton
Cover Design: Niemand Design

Have you ever wondered . . .

Yip-yip-yip-awhooo! A yelping howl echoes through the night. One by one more howlers join in until there's a loud chorus of yips and yelps. Who or what could be making all that noise? It's a group of coyotes "singing" to each other. No one knows what they're saying, but whenever two or more coyotes are in the same neighborhood, chances are there will be some howling.

Howling is the coyote's trademark, but it isn't the only thing coyotes are famous for. They're also known as sly, crafty chicken snatchers and cattle thieves—too fast to be caught, but too much of a problem to be ignored.

Do coyotes deserve this bad reputation? Not entirely. In fact, their main source of food is such small animals as mice and rabbits—the very animals that eat farmers' crops. That makes the coyote both a friend and a foe to farmers. And if coyotes do sometimes attack farm livestock, they are, after all, just doing what they must in order to survive.

Cub Capers

Young coyotes, called *cubs,* like nothing better than to play. If you could sneak up on some coyote brothers and sisters, you'd see some pretty lively action.

One young coyote might be rolling on its back while its brother tugs playfully at an ear. A sister could be tossing a stick high up into the air and trying to catch it. Most of the time she'd probably miss, and the stick might end up landing on her nose!

Not far away you might see another cub trying to sneak up on a squirrel. But just when the cub was about to pounce, the squirrel might bound up a tree and tease the cub with its noisy chatter.

While coyote youngsters play, their mother and father are nearby, keeping watch over the cubs. The parents are ever ready to shoo their family into their *den,* or home, at the first sign of danger.

What lies ahead for these young cubs? How will they learn about hunting, howling, and avoiding enemies? Let's find out.

Opposite page:
The Aztec Indians of Mexico gave the name coyotl *to the animal we know as the coyote. As American settlers moved into the Southwest, the word became part of the English language.*

Coyote Cousins

Coyotes belong to the same family as foxes, Timber Wolves, and dogs. Can you think of some features that all of these animals have in common?

Well, they all have four fairly long legs and fluffy tails. They also have long, thin snouts and sharp, pointed teeth called *canines.*

The coyote's scientific Latin name is *Canis latrans,* which means "barking dog." But the coyote is more like its cousin the Timber Wolf than a dog. Indeed, coyotes look so much like Timber Wolves that they're often mistaken for them. Coyotes sometimes are even called "brush wolves." One way to tell the difference between a coyote and a wolf is to look at the animal's nose and ears. A coyote has a smaller nose pad, and its ears are bigger and more pointed than a wolf's.

Big, pointy ears identify this animal as a coyote.

Coyote or Wolf?

Imagine that you're walking through the woods one late fall afternoon. Out of the corner of your eye you see a brownish-gray animal bounding out of sight. What was it? A coyote? A wolf? If the animal had stayed a moment longer, you might have been able to tell.

One of the big differences between coyotes and wolves is size. Full-grown male coyotes weigh anywhere from 20 to 40 pounds (9 to 18 kilograms). Wolves can be two to three times larger.

But perhaps the easiest way to tell the two animals apart is by their calls. Wolves give one long, sorrowful howl at a time. By contrast, coyotes start with a series of baying yelps or barks, then end with a long, drawn-out howl that sounds like a siren's wail.

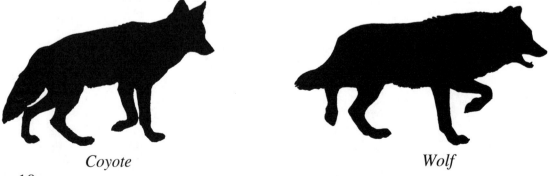

Coyote   *Wolf*

A Successful Survivor

There are 19 kinds of coyotes in North America. Each kind is slightly different in size or color, but all coyotes have one thing in common—they're all very good adapters. In other words, they can change the way they live, including their diets, to make use of what is available.

This gives the coyote an advantage over most animals that can survive only with a certain kind of food or *habitat*—the type of place in which an animal lives naturally. Because the coyote is so good at adapting, it has managed to spread across most of North America. It now has the largest range of any wild animal on the continent.

Where coyotes live in North America

11

Coyote Country

Coyotes seem to feel at home in all kinds of habitats. Forests and parklands as well as grassy meadows provide this adaptable animal with enough cover and food to survive. They even can live on the *tundra,* the flat, treeless plains in arctic regions.

Unlike most animals, coyotes have adjusted to living near people. As the early settlers cleared more and more forests to make farmland, the number of mice and other field-loving animals increased in number. To a coyote, these animals are a yummy meal.

Even though coyotes often live near people and benefit from them, coyotes are shy animals and slightly suspicious of humans. They're also smart enough to stay out of sight. So who knows? If you live in the country, you may have a family of coyotes hunting, playing, and sleeping close by without your even knowing it.

*Coyotes can exist comfortably just about
anywhere—including mountaintops.*

A Warm Coat of Many Colors

Coyotes that live in northern areas where winters are cold grow an extra-thick winter coat that's made up of two layers. The outer layer of coarse *guard hairs* helps to shed rain and snow. Underneath is a thick layer of warm *underfur* that traps body heat next to the animal's skin.

The coyote's coat has four colors. There is lots of *gray* fur on the main part of the coyote's body, with the fur getting darker toward the animal's hind end. Its legs, paws, nose, and the back of the ears are almost *yellow,* and its throat, stomach, and the inside of its ears are *white.* Take a look at the tip of the tail to see the fourth color—*black.*

A coyote's coat changes color with the seasons. To blend in with dark green summer plants, the coyote has a darker coat in that season than the winter. Where a coyote lives also affects its coat color. Mountain coyotes that must blend in with dark shadowy forests tend to be darker than those living in dry desert areas.

Opposite page: *A coyote has a smaller nose pad, but bigger and pointier ears than a wolf.*

Home Territory

Opposite page:
Does this coyote spot something worth pursuing? If it takes chase, this animal's long legs and small feet will enable it to move fast.

Do you have a special route that you always take to a friend's house? Coyotes use special routes all the time. They have well-worn trails that they follow just as you follow the sidewalks and shortcut paths through your neighborhood. But coyotes don't use these routes to visit friends. They use them for hunting. How far a coyote travels while hunting depends on the amount of food available. If there's a lot of food nearby, the coyote's hunting area may be small. If food is scarce, the area will be larger.

The coyote doesn't constantly patrol its *territory*—the area where it lives—to keep out intruders. Instead, it carefully marks the border of the territory to warn other coyotes to stay out. To do this, the coyote sprays certain trees, fence posts, and rock piles with urine and *musk,* a special substance produced by the animal. The strong smell of the musk warns other coyotes that the territory is already taken and that they should move on.

Super Senses

If you looked a coyote right in the face, the first thing you'd notice are its yellow, slightly slanted eyes. They seem to watch your every move. With these crafty-looking, watchful, and alert eyes, it's no wonder that the coyote is considered sly and cunning.

In spite of the coyote's watchful eyes, you'd be surprised to learn that this animal has relatively poor eyesight. It uses its eyes only to detect movement. Fortunately, the coyote's senses of hearing and smell make up for its poor vision.

The coyote's wide, pointed ears are constantly at attention, ready to pick up the slightest sound. And the black, quivering nose at the tip of its long, narrow muzzle can pick up a new smell long before you'd catch a whiff of it.

With its super ears, a coyote can hear a mouse scurrying beneath a foot (about 30 centimeters) of snow.

Dinner on the Move

A coyote needs a good sense of smell and sharp hearing. Why? Its dinner doesn't conveniently come on a plate the way yours does. This animal has to hunt for its food. And the coyote's favorite meals—rabbits, voles, moles, Ground Squirrels, chipmunks, and woodchucks—all move quickly, so the coyote has to be alert and quick, too.

The coyote usually hunts at night and, like many meat-eaters, it *stalks,* or secretly follows, the animals it hunts. While stalking, the coyote moves as quietly as possible. It pads through the countryside, sniffing here, sniffing there. Once in a while the coyote stops and listens intently for any small rustle in the grasses. When it hears or smells food—it pounces!

The coyote's black leather-like nose pad is a protective covering for this animal's sensitive smelling organ.

Share and Share Alike

Sometimes two heads are better than one. Perhaps that's why two coyotes sometimes work together to hunt *prey,* animals hunted by other animals for food. If the coyote team is stalking a rabbit, one coyote attracts the rabbit's attention while the other sneaks up from behind and takes it by surprise. As many as 10 coyotes have been known to hunt as a pack, stalking a larger animal, such as a deer or a pronghorn.

Coyotes will also eat an animal that is already dead. To take advantage of such an opportunity, coyotes keep a careful watch on the sky. If they see vultures soaring, they follow the birds to the place where they land. Chances are that the vultures have spotted and swooped down on a dead animal. The coyotes quickly drive the vultures away and take the free meal for themselves.

When stalking prey, the coyote keeps its body close to the ground. But as it nears its target, the coyote leaps into the air and pounces on the animal.

Tricks of the Trade

Coyotes don't steal food only from vultures. They steal from badgers, too. Badgers often scare mice, squirrels, and pocket gophers out of their *burrows,* or underground homes, by furiously digging into the holes. The coyote knows that the animal inside will try to get away from the badger. Sure enough, the animal pops through an escape hole in its burrow— and pounce!—the coyote has another meal.

The coyote will even "play possum" to attract food. Pretending that it's dead, the coyote waits for a crow to come and investigate. Once the crow is close enough, the coyote leaps up and snatches the unsuspecting bird.

By using these hunting tricks for catching dinner, the clever coyote rarely goes hungry. If all of its tricks should fail and the coyote can't find enough meat, it will eat a wide variety of plants, including fruit and even acorns. When food is plentiful, a coyote travels no more than 5 miles (8 kilometers) a day in search of food. In winter or when food is scarce, the animal has to cover a larger area.

Opposite page:
If this coyote showed you its mouth, you'd see 42 strong teeth that are perfect for grasping, shredding, and tearing food.

Night Concerts

Opposite page:
Though coyotes come out most often at night, they're sometimes seen in the mornings and late afternoons.

Unlike people, coyotes don't need phones to communicate—they *howl* their messages around the countryside.

The urge to contact other coyotes can strike anytime during the night, but usually coyotes do most of their howling at sunrise and sunset.

A coyote usually prefers to howl from a hill. Once it's sitting comfortably high, it throws its head back and lets out its mournful yip-yip-yip-awhoooo. If another coyote is within earshot (and don't forget that coyotes have very sharp hearing), there's sure to be an answering howl. Soon the two coyotes are howling together, and the coyote concert moves on in earnest.

No one is sure why coyotes do so much howling. Sometimes they may be trying to impress a potential mate. Other times they may be warning intruders off their territory. Or they may be teaching their young their amazing howling trick: Coyotes can howl in such a way that the sound seems to come from a much longer way off than it really is.

Silent Signal

Howling isn't the only noise coyotes make. Depending on their mood, they're also good at barking, growling, wailing, and even squealing. But coyotes also send silent messages to each other. How?

Like their cousins Timber Wolves and foxes, coyotes have a hidden scent gland at the base of their tails. A *gland* is a part of an animal's body that makes and gives out a substance. The scent glands of coyotes produce a strong-smelling odor that is slightly different for each animal. By smelling this scent, a coyote can recognize if it belongs to a friend…or an enemy. The process is like your recognizing people by the smell of their perfume or after-shave lotion before you actually see them.

Besides howling, coyotes growl, hiss, whine, and squeal.

All-star Champion

Opposite page:
The coyote gets ready for winter early, growing its thick coat of fur by late September.

Don't ever enter a race with a coyote. You'll lose for sure. An alarmed coyote can reach a speed of 40 miles (64 kilometers) an hour in seconds flat. The coyote's body is built for speed. It has powerful, muscled legs and a slim body, and its doglike paws have claws that give the coyote a good grip on the ground.

Even more amazing is how quickly a coyote can change direction while running full speed. If a sudden noise attracts its attention or if it detects a strange smell, this nimble-footed animal can turn in mid-stride to investigate. Its long, fluffy tail acts as a rudder in the air, balancing the coyote.

The coyote can also swim if necessary. And this animal is an accomplished jumper. When pouncing on a mouse or grasshopper for a snack, the agile coyote can jump more than 12 feet (almost 4 meters). That would be like your leaping over seven school desks and landing on your feet!

Coyote Courtship

Each year around February, coyotes *mate,* or come together, to produce young. The same male and female stay together for life. But if a coyote has never had a mate before or if it has lost its mate, it must try to attract one. How?

Male coyotes have their own version of trying to impress a female. They compete in howling contests! Whoever howls loudest and longest is almost sure to win the female. Sometimes these howling matches end up in a fight. The female in question then gets to choose her mate, most likely the one that she thinks can howl the best. The unsuccessful suitors then start competing all over again for another unattached female while the new couple heads off to start their life together.

This coyote may be alone now—but it probably won't be for long. February is mating time for coyotes.

House Hunting

Opposite page:
A hidden rocky ledge or cave is a fine spot for a coyote den.

After mating, the coyote pair must find a suitable home or den for the babies that will be arriving. Coyotes use dens only when they're raising pups. Choosing and preparing the den is up to the female, but the male helps to get it ready.

The female carefully scouts the *range,* the area where she and her mate live, until she finds a safe and well-hidden location. She'll probably return to the same den year after year.

Coyote parents seldom go to the trouble of digging a den from scratch—even though they're excellent diggers. Why waste time and energy if there might be an abandoned marmot or badger burrow nearby? The coyotes make the old burrow their own by adding some more rooms and corridors until the den is about 9 feet (almost 3 meters) long. This will give their cubs lots of room to romp and wrestle.

As the coyotes enlarge the den, they carefully remove any extra dirt and pile it outside the entrance. Later they spread the loose earth into a heap fanning out from the hole.

An intruder near the den can expect to meet the fierce defense of a mother or father coyote.

Spare Homes

Now that the main den is completed, it's time for the coyote parents to prepare a few more dens. These other dens—and there may be up to 12 of them—are used in emergencies. Now that's thinking ahead! At the first sign of a disturbance around the den or the arrival of an enemy or other threat, the mother moves the babies to another den. Sometimes pups are moved even if there are no problems. Tracks around the den made by the parents and pups make the den easy to spot by *predators,* animals that hunt other animals for food. Having other dens for a quick getaway ensures the cubs' safety.

When looking for additional dens, sometimes the coyote mother can't find an old, unused burrow. Then she'll have to make do with a hole at the base of a big old tree or between some giant boulders. Or she may search out a dark and dry cave, a hollow log, or even a deserted shack or drainpipe.

Overleaf:
These cubs are definitely more than one month old. That's the age at which cubs start to explore the world outside their den.

Cuddly Cubs

Before her babies are born in spring or early summer, the female thoroughly cleans the den to make it tidy and comfy for the new arrivals.

Usually five to seven cubs are born, but there's one recorded case of 19 babies in a *litter,* the baby animals that are born together. The tiny new coyotes have limp, floppy ears; a fuzzy covering of woolly hair; and a long, black stripe running down their backs. In fact, you could easily mistake them for newborn puppies. They have pushed-in noses and they make soft whimpering sounds. As with many animal babies, their eyes are tightly closed and won't open for as long as two weeks.

For the first month, the cubs live solely by *nursing*—drinking milk from their mother's body. Then they're gradually given less milk and they start eating meat. At first they can't handle the hunks of meat that their father brings to the den. So the mother chews and partly digests the meat, then brings up the softened meat and feeds it to her babies. But in no time, the fast-growing cubs are ready to handle big chunks of meat on their own.

Two pups poke their heads out of their dark burrow and into the sunshine.

Keeping Babies Safe

After a month, the cubs are now allowed to go just outside the den entrance. They spend much of the day snoozing or romping around, but their mother is always close by and always alert for danger. If she senses a prowling lynx, bear, wolf, or other predator, she gives a special warning yelp. Quickly the obedient cubs head for the safety of the den.

If the predator doesn't go away, the anxious mother may even fake a limp to distract the predator. Off she stumbles, luring the enemy away from the den. Once she's satisfied that her cubs are safe, her "sore leg" suddenly is magically healed, and she races back to the den. The confused enemy is probably left wondering whether it had just dreamed the whole strange episode!

A coyote mother is always on the alert for enemies.

Dutiful Dad

Cubs meet their father for the first time when they leave the den. Before that they're cared for only by their mother. But if the cubs didn't actually see their father, he wasn't very far away. All along he's been faithfully prowling outside the den, making sure his brand new family is safe and secure. He's also been in charge of bringing food to the mother coyote. Without his deposits of meat at the den's entrance hole, she could not have eaten and, in turn, given her cubs all the care and milk they needed in those early days.

Once the cubs emerge from the den, both the mother and the father look after them. The parents' most important job is to teach the young ones how to hunt.

The cubs start their hunting lessons with something small—a grasshopper, perhaps. They learn how to stalk and pounce, and then they move on to bigger prey—mice and voles. The cubs also learn which animals are their enemies and where to find shelter in stormy weather. In short, they learn all the skills they'll need to know for staying alive.

Coyote parents and young form a close family unit while the cubs are growing up.

On Their Own

By fall the young coyotes start to leave their parents and search for their own territories. Thanks to the careful training they received, they're ready to be self-sufficent. They can hunt and howl, and when they reach one year of age, they'll be ready to pick a mate.

No doubt young coyotes will face many dangers. They must be careful to avoid Timber Wolves and Grizzly Bears because both are large enough to kill the smaller-size coyote. Among their other, smaller enemies are cougars and Golden Eagles.

But coyotes are clever, and with a bit of luck, the well-trained youngsters will live for eight to ten years in the wild. During that time, they'll raise several coyote families of their own.

Words To Know

Burrow   A hole in the ground dug by an animal to use as a home.

Canines   Sharp, pointed teeth.

Cubs   Young coyotes.

Den   An animal home.

Gland   A part of an animal's body that makes and gives out a substance.

Guard hairs   Long, coarse hairs that make up the outer layer of a coyote's coat.

Habitat   The type of place in which an animal naturally lives.

Litter   Young animals born together.

Mate   To come together to produce young. Either member of an animal pair is also called the other's mate.

Musk   A powerful-smelling substance produced by an animal to mark its territory and attract a mate.

Nurse   To drink milk from the mother's body.

Predator   An animal that hunts other animals for food.

Prey   An animal hunted by another animal for food.

Range   The area an animal lives in.

Stalk   To follow prey quietly and stealthily.

Territory   The area an animal lives in and defends from other animals of the same kind.

Tundra   Flat, treeless land in arctic regions.

Underfur   Thick, short hair that traps body-warmed air next to an animal's skin.

Index

Getting To Know...

Nature's Children

SPIDERS

Bill Ivy

SCHOLASTIC INC.

New York Toronto London Auckland Sydney
Mexico City New Delhi Hong Kong Buenos Aires

Facts in Brief

Classification of North American spiders

Class: *Arachnida* (spiders, scorpions, ticks and mites)

Order: *Araneae* (spiders)

Family: There are 23 families of spiders in North America.

Genus: 116 genera of spiders are represented in North America.

Species: Approximately 220 species of spiders are found in North America.

World distribution. Varies with species.

Habitat. Varies with species.

Distinctive physical characteristics. Eight legs, two-part body, spinnerets on abdomen.

Habits. Spin silken webs and threads for a variety of uses; lay eggs in silken sacs which are sometimes abandoned and sometimes guarded or hidden, depending upon the particular habits of the species.

Diet. Mainly body juices of animals, usually insects.

Published by Scholastic Inc.
90 Old Sherman Turnpike, Danbury, Connecticut 06816.

SCHOLASTIC and associated logos are trademarks of Scholastic Inc.

ISBN 0-7172-6706-7   Printed in the U.S.A.

Have you ever wondered . . .

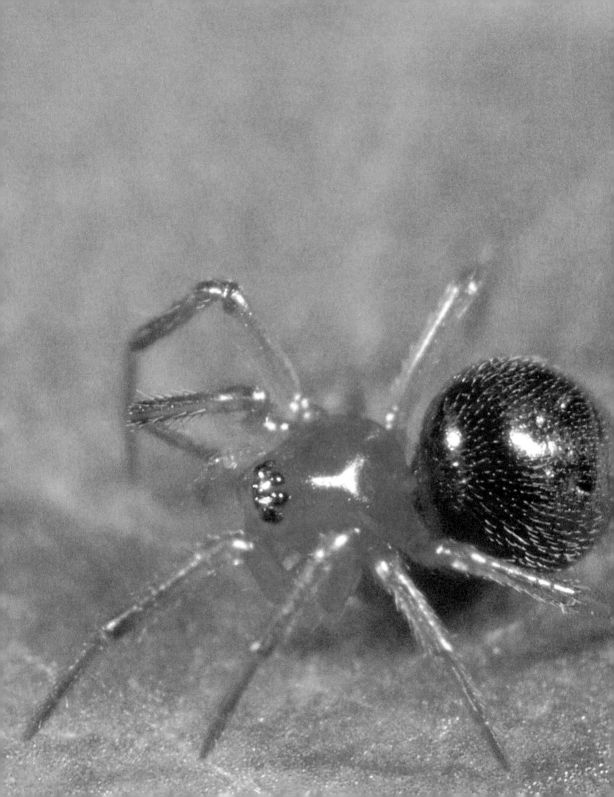

"Along came a spider
Who sat down beside her
And frightened Miss Muffet away."

Everyone knows the old rhyme and most people are about as fond of spiders as Miss Muffet was. If a spider sat down next to you, what would you do? Many people would run away or even kill it. This is a shame because spiders do not deserve such a bad reputation. They do far more good than harm. They are gifted athletes, architects, weavers, hunters, pilots and performers. You may be surprised to learn how talented and fascinating spiders really are. Are you curious?

The Dwarf Spider is so tiny that four or five would fit on the nail of your baby finger.

Spidery Homes

If you wanted to find a spider, where would you look? In a field, in the woods, on a beach or in a house? You could search in any one of these places and you would probably be successful. Spiders of many shapes and sizes can be found, some on the highest mountains and some in the lowest valleys. Some even live in the water!

Spiders are very common. Over 3000 different species live in North America. Worldwide, more than 35,000 species have been identified. But scientists have not yet looked for spiders in all the places spiders can live. They suspect that their job is only half done and that there are probably at least another 35,000 species waiting to be discovered.

Who is What?

Did you know that a spider is not an insect? At first glance, spiders and insects look very similar, but they are really very different. Insects have six legs, three body parts and antennae. Usually they also have a set of wings, at least at some time in their lives. Spiders, on the other hand, have eight legs and two body parts, plus a pair of palpi—feelers that look like two short legs. They never have wings or antennae.

Spiders and insects belong to different classes of animals. Spiders, as well as mites, ticks and scorpions, are Arachnids. One familiar Arachnid, the Daddy Longlegs, is a spider look-alike. Don't be fooled! Daddy may have eight legs, but he has only one body part.

Opposite page:

Long-legged spiders like this one are rather clumsy and slower than those with shorter legs.

Anatomy of a Spider

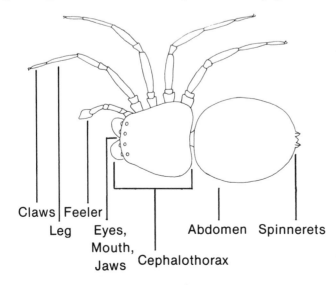

Claws | Feeler

Leg Eyes, Abdomen Spinnerets
     Mouth,
     Jaws Cephalothorax

9

Silk Spinners

To us, silk is a luxury. To a spider, it is a necessity. A spider uses its silk to get its food, to build its shelter, to protect its eggs and to travel safely.

Spiders' silk is an amazing material. A single strand is extremely fine, but it is also extremely strong. In fact, a steel wire of the same thickness cannot match its strength.

A number of special glands inside the spider's abdomen produce liquid silk. The silk flows from the spider's body through spinnerets near the back of its undersides. Lines of silk come out of tiny holes on the tip of each spinneret, join together and harden into a single, fine thread. Different silk glands make different kinds of silk. Some make dry strands, others sticky. Some make very fine strands, others thicker. As the spider works, it chooses just the right thread for the job it is doing.

Wherever a spider goes, it leaves a trail of silk behind it. This silken "drag-line" can help the spider retrace its steps, and it may even save its life.

Opposite page:

Look closely and you will see this Jumping Spider's drag-line.

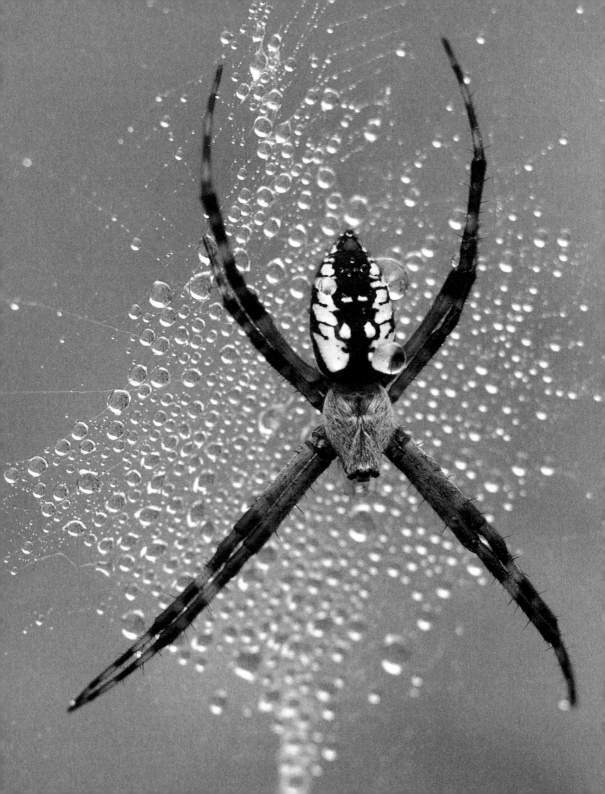

Master Weavers

" 'Come into my parlor,' said the spider to the fly." For the unfortunate insect that blunders into the spider's "parlor," the first visit is usually the last. Of course, spiders do not really have parlors, but most do spend their days sitting in or near the intricate webs they weave. The webs may seem beautiful or messy to us, but they are deadly traps for unwary insects.

When it comes to web building, the orb-weaving spiders are in a class of their own. These spiders are very common and come in various shapes, sizes and colors. Look for their webs in your garden. There is usually one there.

You may have to look carefully. Most of the time, the orb-weavers' wagonwheel webs are almost invisible. But on dew-drenched mornings, these masterpieces glisten in the sun. You might think they would take hours to create but in fact they usually take less than one hour.

Orb-weaving spiders often hang upside-down in the center of their webs.

Insects get stuck in spider webs because many of the web's silk threads are sticky. So why doesn't the spider get stuck too? The spider uses different threads when it builds its web. In an orb web, it uses dry thread for the spokes and the central look-out and sticky thread for the circles. The spider always knows which is which. But just in case it misses its step, slippery oil on the spider's feet seems to give it extra protection.

Orb web construction.
1. *The spider releases a thread of silk which is carried by the wind forming a bridge.*
2. *Next the spider drops on a thread to a base below.*
3. *A strand from the bridge is pulled down to form the letter Y.*
4. *The spider backtracks, attaches a new thread to the centre hub, then carries it into position.*
5. *This process is repeated until the web frame is completed (6).*
7. *A spiral of sticky silk is then added.*
8. *Finished web.*

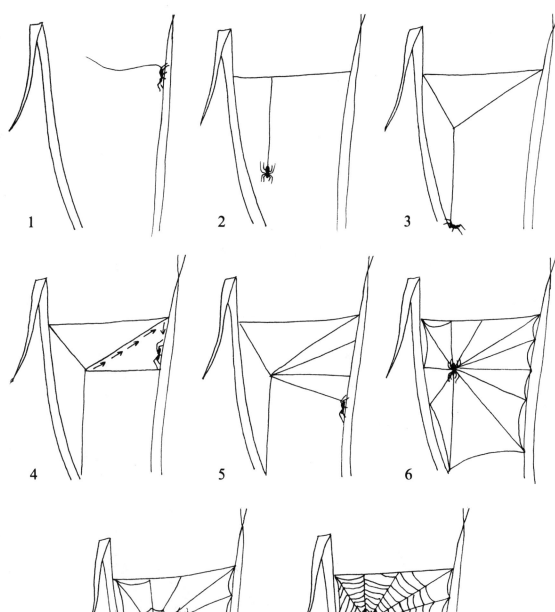

1   2   3
4   5   6
7   8

Terrible Eyesight, Terrific Touch

If you were to study the face of a spider under a magnifying glass, the first thing you would notice would be as many as eight eyes staring right back at you! Some spiders have two rows of eyes, while others have three. These may be grouped close together or spread widely apart. Exactly how these eyes are arranged helps to identify different species of spider.

You would think that with so many eyes, spiders would have excellent vision. But most do not. All spiders that trap their prey are extremely short-sighted. Only spiders that hunt have good eyesight.

Fortunately for trapping spiders, their sense of touch is much better developed than their sight. A trapping spider does not need to see its prey. It can feel the vibrations of an insect struggling in its web. And it can tell exactly where the insect is by feeling where there is extra pull on the threads of its web.

"Here's looking at you, kid!"

Talented Trappers

Not all web-spinners live in their webs. Some set up house in the leaves nearby. A thick thread of silk leads from their shelter to their web and works like a telephone line. If any insect should get trapped, the web and the line will vibrate as it struggles to get away. The spider always keeps one foot on the line, and with its strong sense of touch, it can always tell when dinner is served.

One family of spiders builds a funnel-shaped web that opens out into a wide sheet of tangled silk. Several silk strands hang overhead and trip up unsuspecting passersby while the spider waits patiently inside the funnel's narrow tube.

Trapping insects is hard on the web. Most spiders spin a fresh one each night. Others, however, are content with a simple patch job, so long as there are enough sticky threads to make the day's catch.

A funnel-weaving spider greets its unlucky dinner guests.

Soup's On

When an unfortunate insect happens to fly into a web, the spider dashes out to make its catch. Using very fine, dry silk, it wraps its prey like a mummy. At the same time, it uses its sharp, curved fangs to inject its victim with a paralyzing venom. In a matter of minutes, its prey is helpless. If the spider is not very hungry, it will hang its parcel of food from its web and save it for a midnight snack.

No matter when they eat, spiders have a very unusual way of eating. They do not chew their food. They drink it! A spider's mouth is small and toothless and only good for sucking. Fortunately, the spider can produce its digestive juices *before* it eats. These juices turn its food into a tasty soup that only a spider could love. Insect broth is its usual diet, but some large fishing spiders may even dine on fish chowder.

Spider webs come in all sizes, shapes and patterns, from simple to fancy.

Trap-door Spider at home.

Accomplished Architects

Not all spiders snare their food with a web. One accomplished architect, the tiny Trap-door Spider, builds a different kind of trap.

Using its fangs as a shovel, this spider digs a hole in the ground. It then plasters this tunnel with a mixture of sand and saliva that is completely waterproof once it dries. Next, this careful builder lines its cozy home with silk. Saving the best for last, it constructs a door complete with a silk hinge at one end. This shuts out the cold and damp and keeps the spider safe when it wants to nap.

When the Trap-door Spider is hungry, it leaves the door ajar and patiently waits for an insect to pass by. In the blink of an eye, it rushes out and pulls its victim inside.

Should any unwanted intruders come near, it slams the door shut and hangs on for dear life! Its grip is so strong you would need a knife to pry the door open.

A Nursery-web Spider waits patiently to catch an insect or a minnow.

A-Hunting We Will Go

Not all spiders rely on chance to bring prey to their traps. Some, such as the Wolf Spider, go searching for it. Like the wolf it is named after, the Wolf Spider is a skillful, keen-eyed hunter. Once it spots its prey the chase is on. It is an excellent sprinter, and few insects are fast enough to escape with their lives.

The Bolas Spider hunts at night and uses a very unusual method. It does not spin a web or run down its prey. Instead it uses a kind of lasso. First, the Bolas Spider makes a sticky ball and fastens it to the end of a silk thread. Then it waits. When a moth flies by, it hurls the lasso into the air so that it tangles up its victim's wings and legs. One lucky strike takes care of dinner tonight!

Wolf Spider.

Super Athletes

Many spiders are good acrobats, but none can match the athletic skill of the Jumping Spider. This tiny gymnast can jump forty times its own length. A tall man would have to leap the length of a city block to match that feat.

Jumping Spiders put this skill to good use. Since they spin no webs, they must hunt for their food. Silently they stalk their prey. At just the right moment, they pounce. Thanks to their excellent eyesight, they rarely miss.

Being a silk-spinner sometimes makes hunting easier. When a Jumping Spider spots an insect from a high perch, it quickly anchors a drag-line before it leaps. Then, whether it catches its prey or not, it has a silken ladder leading straight back up to its perch.

Ready to pounce!

Deadly Disguise

While most spiders are hard to see in their habitats, none can match the vanishing act of Crab Spiders. These camouflage artists seem to disappear into their surroundings. Many actually change color, though it takes them a few days to do so.

This ability comes in handy. Many Crab Spiders hide on flowers and become the same bright color as the petals. Any insect landing on a blossom to feed is in for a big surprise!

How the Crab Spider got its name is no mystery. Not only does it look like a crab, it moves like one too. It can run backwards or sideways with ease.

This Crab Spider spends most of its time hiding in flowers. It is therefore known—you guessed it!—as the Flower Spider.

Risky Business

When the male spider is fully grown, it begins its search for a mate. Finding her is easy, but approaching her is not. The female spider is usually much larger than the male, and she may be more interested in him as a meal than as a partner.

The males of each species have their own ways of getting a female's attention. Some do a dance while others twang and drum on her web. One even presents the female with a tasty gift of insect wrapped in silk.

If the female is agreeable, the male approaches and they mate. However, after mating the male usually beats a hasty retreat. His mate is not moved by tender feelings. She could still change her mind and eat him for dinner.

This attractive spider makes its home in a rolled-up leaf.

Small Beginnings

Do you know the saying, "Don't put all your eggs in one basket"? Well, that is exactly what most female spiders do. They weave lovely silk baskets to cradle their jelly-like eggs. These baskets are called egg sacs or cocoons.

Because spider eggs make a fine meal for many of the spider's enemies, spider mothers try to find safe places to hide them. Some try to camouflage their cocoon by covering it with dead leaves or twigs. Others hang it in the web during the day. They keep a watchful eye on it and at night they even take it to bed with them.

The most protective spider mothers take no chances. They attach their cocoon to their body and never leave home without it. Sometimes an egg sac is so big the mother has to walk on tiptoe to keep it from dragging! No matter how careful she is, the cocoon takes many bumps. If it falls off, she stops abruptly and reattaches it. If it rolls out of sight, she searches for it frantically. And if her precious package is threatened, she fights fiercely to defend it.

Opposite page:

The female Wolf Spider keeps her egg sac attached to her abdomen and guards it fearlessly.

Can You Count the Spiderlings?

Spiders have very large families. Imagine having hundreds or even thousands of brothers and sisters! Is it any wonder spider families do not stay together for very long?

Baby spiders, or spiderlings, are miniature versions of their parents, except that they are colorless and have no markings. Most go off their separate ways as soon as they hatch. Within a few days some can even build their own webs, although these are not as fancy as their mothers'. Other spiderlings stay close to home. When they are no larger than a grain of sand, they build mini-burrows next door to mom's.

Some spiderlings need their mother's care for a time after they hatch. The female Nursery-web Spider builds a special tent to house her young and then carefully watches over them. The female Wolf Spider carries her spiderlings with her, piggyback. The ride is quite rough, and some spiderlings fall off. But that is all right. They can usually hitch a ride on the next mother to pass by. Wolf Spiders do not mind. There is always room for one more.

Opposite page:

Hatch-day.

Little Astronauts

What has eight legs, no wings and flies? Give up? Believe it or not, the answer is a spider!

To fly without wings, spiders use a method known as ballooning. Little spiderlings are the real experts at this sport.

To balloon, a spiderling climbs up as high as possible on a plant or fence post. Facing into the wind, it spins one or more long strands of silk known as gossamer. The wind catches these strands like a kite and carries them and the light-weight spiderlings high into the air.

Most spiderlings do not go very far, but some may travel great distances. Pilots have reported seeing these little astronauts as high up as 4200 metres (14,000 feet). Others have been seen over 300 kilometres (200 miles) out at sea.

Once they touch down, the spiderlings discard their parachutes and explore their new surroundings. If they do not like what they find, they soar off again in search of a better home. Sometimes hundreds of young spiders balloon together and whole fields are covered with their gossamer.

Opposite page:

Quite a balancing act!

36

Bigger and Bigger Coats

What a curious creature the spider is! There is not a single bone in its body. Instead, it has a hard outer covering known as an exoskeleton. This acts like a suit of armor and helps protect it.

The exoskeleton, however, does not stretch, and as a spider grows, it becomes a pretty snug fit! If you wear a coat that is too small, it will tear at the seams. This is exactly what happens to a growing spider's covering. The old skeleton splits down the back and the spider struggles to pull itself out. It is no easy task freeing all those legs!

The spider's fresh skeleton is ready and waiting beneath the old one. At first it is weak and soft, but it soon becomes as hard as the one just shed.

This change of clothes is called molting. It may take place up to ten times before the spider is fully grown.

No, you are not seeing double. This tarantula has just shed its skin.

A Hard Life

Life is very dangerous for a spider. It must be constantly on the lookout for hungry frogs, toads, birds, mammals, fish—and even other spiders. No creature can be trusted, not even its own kind.

Some insects prey on spiders as well. The Praying Mantis, for one, catches the spider with speed. It strikes even more quickly than the spider. But most deadly of all are tiny flies and wasps that lay their eggs in or on the spider's body. In time the grubs hatch and dine on their unfortunate host. As often happens in the natural world, the hunter has become the hunted.

This Nursery-web Spider has prepared a silken home for her hatchlings.

Gentle Giants

Spiders have a bad reputation. Do they really deserve it?

Meet the King Kong of the spider world, the strong, hairy tarantula. Its body often grows to be 7 centimetres (almost 3 inches) long and its legs often measure 8 centimetres (over 3 inches). It is the largest spider in North America.

But looks can be deceiving. Tarantulas are not the villains they are often made out to be. If a North American tarantula bit you, it would only be about as serious and painful as a bee sting.

In truth trantulas are very timid creatures. They live in the desert, spending their days underground and usually coming out to hunt only at night. Their eyesight is very poor and they rely on their sense of touch to guide them.

The Red-legged Tarantula may live up to fifteen years.

Dynamic Duo

Of all the spiders in North America, only two are dangerous: the Brown Recluse and the Black Widow. Neither of these shy spiders likes to bite, but if disturbed, they may strike.

The Brown Recluse lives only in the southern United States. It is also known as the Fiddleback because of a violin-shaped marking on the back of its head. Luckily its bite almost never kills, though it does hurt and is slow to heal.

The Black Widow, however, can kill. Only the female bites and her venom is the most potent in the world. Still, most people who are bitten live to tell the tale.

The Black Widow is easy to spot. It is jet black with a red hourglass marking on its belly. Since the female often eats the male after mating, she has certainly earned her name.

Female Black Widow.

Your Friend, The Spider

Spiders—even the ones which can hurt us—are our friends. They kill billions of insects, many of which carry disease and destroy our plants. They are a natural form of pest control.

At one time, doctors even thought spiders were good for the health! They prescribed spiders and their webs as a cure for fever. That is not as crazy as it sounds. Scientists have since discovered that spiderwebs actually do contain a fever-reducing drug.

Now that you know a little more about spiders, perhaps you won't be afraid of them. Enjoy the sight of their orb webs glistening in the morning sun. Take time to watch them travel from spoke to spoke on their webs or wrap a freshly caught insect in silk. Spiders are almost always harmless and very helpful too.

Words To Know

Arachnids   Members of the class *Arachnida:* spiders, scorpions, ticks and mites.

Ballooning   A method of travel used by young spiders: they float through the air hanging from silken threads that are carried by the wind.

Camouflage   Markings or coloring that help an animal blend into the background.

Cocoon   A case spun by spiders to protect their eggs. Also called egg sac.

Drag-line   A silken line made and used by spiders to secure them to one spot.

Exoskeleton   The hard outer covering of a spider's body.

Gland   A part of an animal's body that produces a substance; the spider's silk is made by glands.

Gossamer   Threads small spiders spin in order to balloon.

Grubs   Name given to insects in the second stage of their development.

Habitat   An animal's natural home.

Mate   To come together to produce young. Either member of an animal pair is also the other's mate.

Molting   The shedding of a spider's exoskeleton.

Palpi   The name given to spiders' feelers.

Prey   An animal hunted by another animal for food.

Spiderling   A baby spider.

Spinnerets   The organs used by spiders to spin their webs and lines.

Venom   A poisonous fluid.

INDEX

Cover Photo: Bill Ivy
Photo Credits: Bill Ivy, pages 4, 7, 8, 11, 12, 16, 20, 23, 25, 26, 29, 30, 33, 34, 37, 38, 41, 43; Robert McCaw (Network Stock Photo File), 19; S.J. Krasemann (Valan Phots), 44.